Lerner SPORTS

BRAZIL NATIONAL SOCCER TEAMS

ULTIMATE FAN GUIDE

JANIE SCHEFFER

Lerner Publications ◆ Minneapolis

To Dad and Katie—you will always be my Pelé and Mia Hamm.

Lerner Publications Company
An imprint of Lerner Publishing Group, Inc.
241 First Avenue North
Minneapolis, MN 55401 USA

For reading levels and more information, look up this title at www.lernerbooks.com.

Main body text set in Aptifer Slab LT Pro.
Typeface provided by Linotype AG.

Editor: Evan Villas **Designer:** Viet Chu **Photo Editor:** Cynthia Zemlicka
Lerner team: Sue Marquis

Library of Congress Cataloging-in-Publication Data

Names: Scheffer, Janie, 1992– author
Title: Brazil national soccer teams : ultimate fan guide / Janie Scheffer.
Description: Minneapolis : Lerner Publications, [2026] | Series: Lerner Sports. World Cup fan guides | Includes bibliographical references and index. | Audience: Ages 7–11 | Audience: Grades 2–3 | Summary: "From Marta to Pelé, Brazil is home to one of the best national soccer teams in the world. Explore the men and women and the many World Cup and Olympic victories of this legendary team"— Provided by publisher.
Identifiers: LCCN 2025011878 | ISBN 9798765689370 lib. bdg. | ISBN 9798348029296 pbk | ISBN 9798765698587 epub
Subjects: LCSH: Copa América (Tournament) | World Cup (Soccer) | Soccer—Brazil—History—Juvenile literature | Soccer players—Brazil—Anecdotes | Soccer fans—Brazil—Juvenile literature | Olympics—History—Juvenile literature

Classification: LCC GV944.B7 S34 2026 | DDC 796.3340981—dc23/eng/20250818
LC record available at https://lccn.loc.gov/2025011878

Manufactured in the United States of America
1-1012735-54805-8/12/2025

TABLE OF CONTENTS

INTRODUCTION
1970 WORLD CHAMPIONS 4

CHAPTER 1
THE COUNTRY OF FOOTBALL 8

CHAPTER 2
FIVE-TIME WORLD CHAMPIONS 15

CHAPTER 3
PASSIONATE PLAYERS AND FANS 25

BRAZIL WOMEN'S TEAM TIMELINE 28

BRAZIL MEN'S TEAM TIMELINE..................... 29

GLOSSARY.. 30

LEARN MORE......................................31

INDEX.. 32

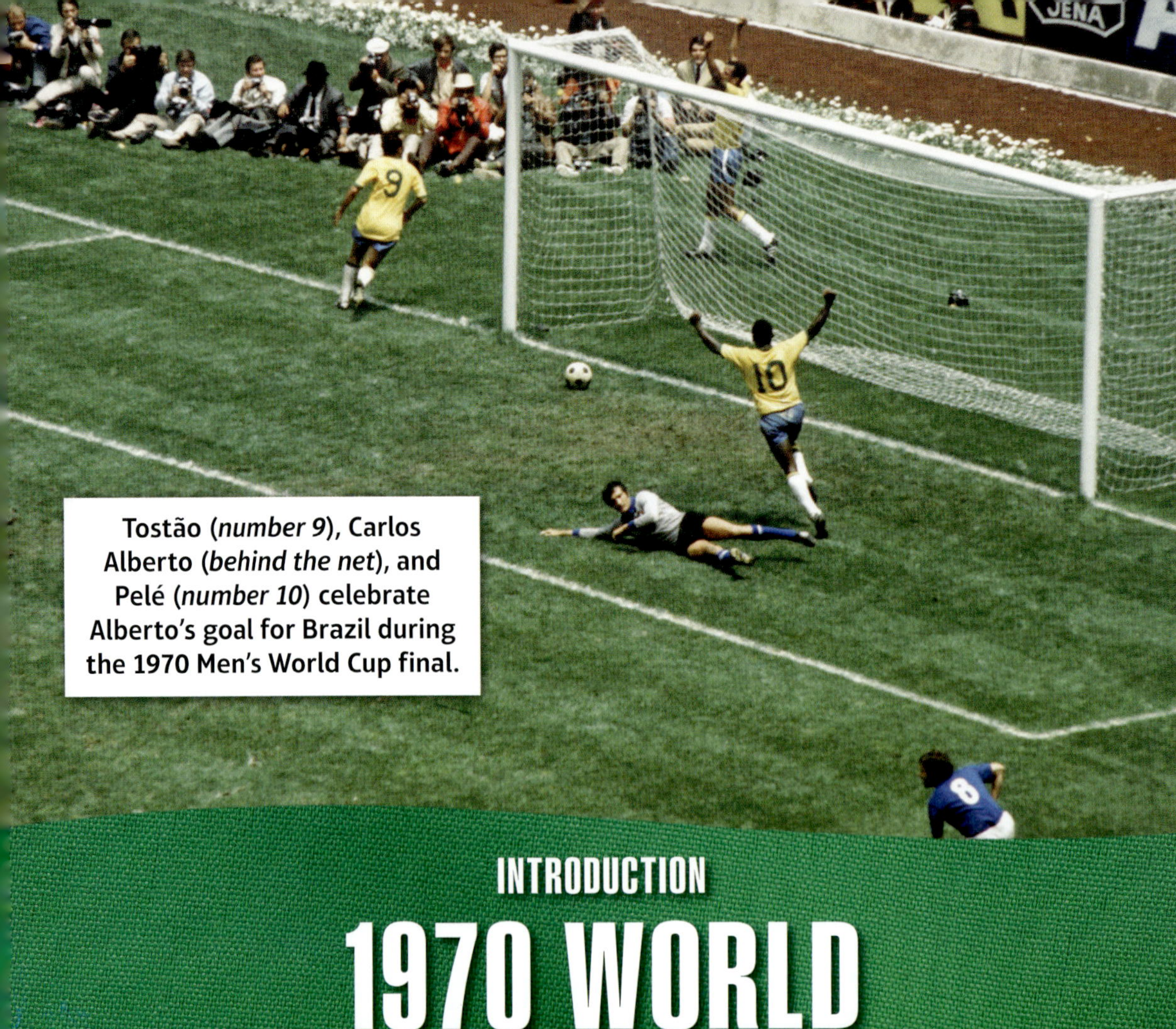

Tostão (*number 9*), Carlos Alberto (*behind the net*), and Pelé (*number 10*) celebrate Alberto's goal for Brazil during the 1970 Men's World Cup final.

INTRODUCTION

1970 WORLD CHAMPIONS

Passionate soccer fans were packed into Estadio Azteca in Mexico City, Mexico, to watch the final match of the 1970 Men's World Cup. As the game clock ran down, Italy's fans and players were losing hope. Brazil led Italy 3–1. In the 86th minute of play, Brazil was ready to strike again.

With their precise passing, Brazil worked their way up the field. Brazil's superstar Pelé made an expert pass to team captain Carlos Alberto, and Alberto buried the ball in the bottom corner of the net. Goal! Brazil had just sealed their third Men's World Cup title. This 1970 team was the best national team in Brazil's history.

Men's and women's national soccer teams are made up of the most talented players from the country. Both teams dream of claiming the World Cup trophy. FIFA organizes this competition. Different countries host it every four years.

FAST FACTS

The golden age of Brazil soccer began in 1958 with Brazil's first Men's World Cup title.

A long-standing ban on women's soccer kept a women's program from developing in Brazil for many years.

Pelé played his first Men's World Cup in 1958 at 17 years old.

Marta won the Best FIFA Women's Player award six times.

Pelé (*second from left*) playing in the 1970 Men's World Cup final

Brazil also competes every four years in the Summer Olympics. They face other South American teams in the Copa América tournament every four years. In most countries, soccer is called *football*. Brazil has earned its nickname as the Country of Football.

Marta (*right*) controls the ball during the gold medal match at the 2024 Olympics.

Brazil's men's team played in the first World Cup in 1930.

CHAPTER 1

THE COUNTRY OF FOOTBALL

The first men's national team in Brazil formed in 1914. It was made up of players from two Brazilian cities: São Paulo and Rio de Janeiro. The team started off strong. It won both the 1919 and 1922 South American Championship, which was later named Copa América.

Arthur Friedenreich, an incredible striker, led Brazil to both victories on their home field. But then came a long losing streak. Brazil did not win any major title for 27 years.

Brazil striker Arthur Friedenreich in 1921

In 1949, Brazil won the South American Championship at home. This victory brought hope for the team and its fans. One year later, Brazil hosted the Men's World Cup. They made it all the way to the final match against Uruguay, but they lost 2–1. Uruguay came from behind to take the Men's World Cup title.

Brazil's men's team ahead of their first match at the 1950 World Cup

Pelé plays in his first World Cup in 1958.

The next decade of Brazilian soccer included some major changes. Team colors changed to yellow, blue, and green. Coach Vicente Feola enforced stricter team rules. Then Pelé made his debut on the team in 1957. The golden age of Brazil soccer began with Brazil's first Men's World Cup title in 1958 and lasted for the next 20 years.

WORLD CUP WINNERS

Brazil's men's national team is one of the most successful teams in Men's World Cup history. They have won the tournament five times!

Women's soccer in Brazil began to take off in the 1980s. A women's team had appeared in international friendly matches before this. But a long-standing ban on women's soccer kept the program from developing. It took many years for the country to accept and support women's soccer.

The Brazil women's national team played its first official match in 1986 against the United States. Brazil lost 2–1, but it was a breakthrough moment for women's soccer in the country. It also kick-started a rivalry with the United States that continues to this day.

Brazil's women's team lines up before a game at the 1996 Olympics.

Formiga celebrates her game-winning goal during Brazil's third-place Women's World Cup match in 1999.

In 1991, Brazil's women's team played in the first Women's World Cup and took ninth place. As interest in women's soccer grew, so did the strength of Brazil's team. Just eight years later, Brazil took third place in the Women's World Cup. Midfielder Miraildes Maciel Mota, better known as Formiga, made the final penalty kick of the game to secure the third-place finish.

Marta scores a goal during a 2007 Women's World Cup match.

Brazil's strength grew with key players such as Marta. Her impressive goals earned her the FIFA Best Women's Player of the Year award six times. Marta helped the team win a silver Olympic medal in 2004 and a second-place finish at the 2007 Women's World Cup. In both competitions, longtime rivals Brazil, the United States, and Germany battled for the top three spots.

Ronaldo (*center*) scores a goal in a match against Turkey at the Men's World Cup in 2002.

CHAPTER 2

FIVE-TIME WORLD CHAMPIONS

Brazil's men's team is nicknamed Canarinho, or little canary, for the canary yellow color of their jerseys. The team dominates the Men's World Cup stage. Brazil won the event in 1958, 1962, 1970, 1994, and 2002.

Pelé, one of the greatest soccer players of all time, led the team to Men's World Cup victories in 1958, 1962, and 1970. At just 17 years old, Pelé began the 1958 event on the bench. But during a 0–0 tied match, Brazil's coach, Vicente Feola, gave Pelé a chance. Within the first three minutes of play, Pelé took a shot and hit the goalpost.

Like Pelé (*right*), many famous Brazilians are known by a single name.

Pelé (*left*) heads the ball during the 1970 Men's World Cup final.

From that moment on, Pelé took over. In the next three games, he scored six goals to secure Brazil's first Men's World Cup title. Pelé's six goals earned him three Men's World Cup records: youngest goal scorer, youngest hat-trick scorer, and youngest final match scorer.

An injury kept Pelé from playing a key role in Brazil's 1962 Men's World Cup title. Manuel Francisco dos Santos stepped up in his place. Dos Santos, known as Garrincha, scored four goals leading up to their final match victory.

Brazil's men's team at the 1970 World Cup final

Brazil's best national team ever took the Men's World Cup pitch in 1970. They faced Italy in the final match. Fans call soccer the Beautiful Game. Brazil's key players Pelé, Garrincha, Jairzinho, Gerson, Tostão, Rivellino, and Alberto played the game with beauty.

Pelé scored the first goal. By halftime, Italy had tied the game 1–1. Brazil responded in the second half with goals by Gerson, Jairzinho, and Alberto to win their third Men's World Cup title.

Pelé retired from the national team after the 1970 World Cup. Brazil entered a time of rebuilding. By the 1994 Men's World Cup, the team regained its strength. They beat Italy in penalty kicks to win their fourth Word Cup title.

Then came "The Three Rs": Ronaldo, Rivaldo, and Ronaldinho. In the 2002 Men's World Cup they were an unstoppable trio. Ronaldinho scored on a penalty kick that secured their semifinal win against England. Ronaldo netted eight goals during the tournament. Two of them came in the final game against Germany. Brazil won their fifth Men's World Cup title.

Ronaldo (*right*) scores a goal during the 2002 World Cup final.

In 2010, Brazil had a new star player: Neymar. A goal-scoring ace, Neymar helped the team win their first Olympic gold medal in 2016. Brazil's victory came down to a penalty kick by Neymar. Three years later, forward Everton Soares led the team to its ninth Copa América title. He scored three goals in the tournament.

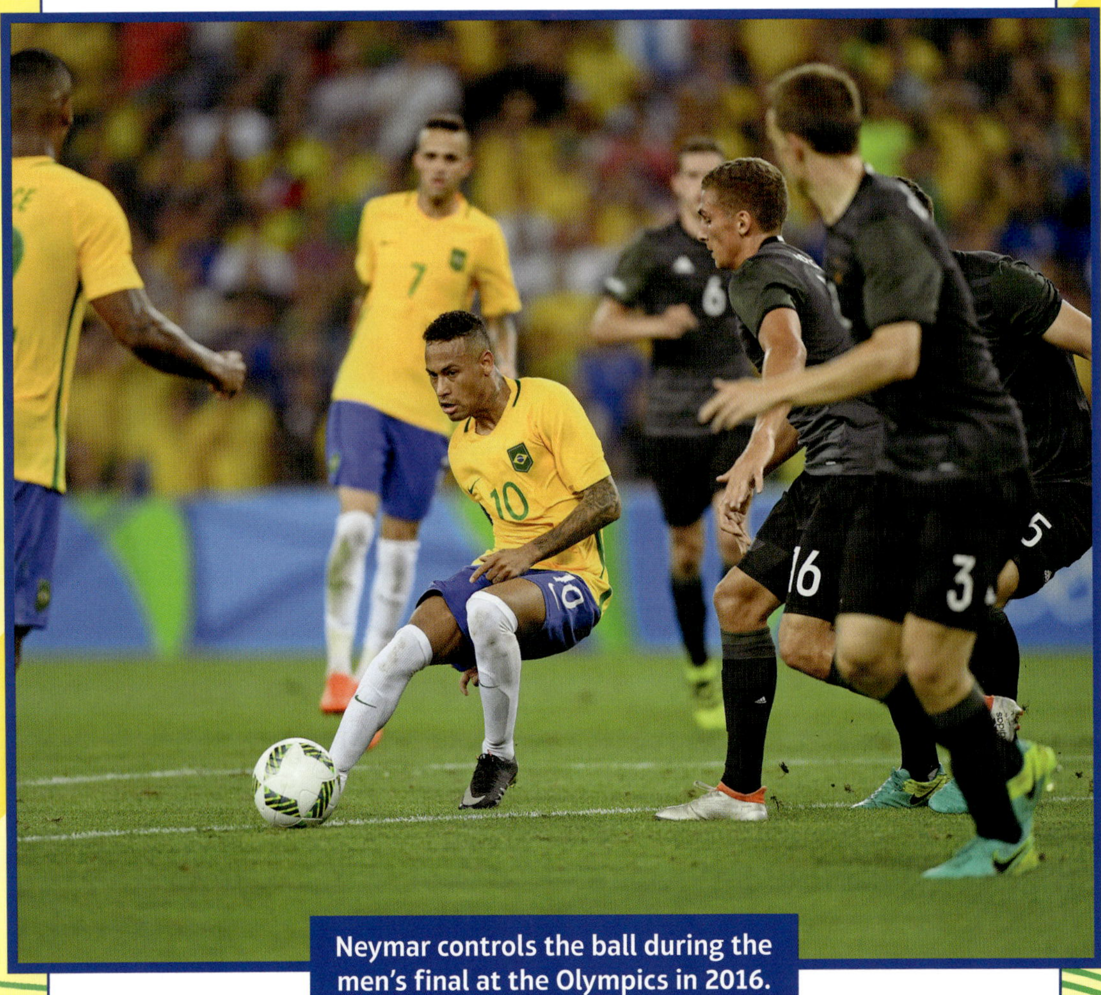

Neymar controls the ball during the men's final at the Olympics in 2016.

Sissi playing in the third-place match at the 1999 Women's World Cup

Brazil's women's team has also found World Cup success. In a 1999 game against Nigeria, Brazil's star midfielder Sissi scored the game-winning goal in overtime. Sissi's goal is considered one of the greatest moments in Women's World Cup history.

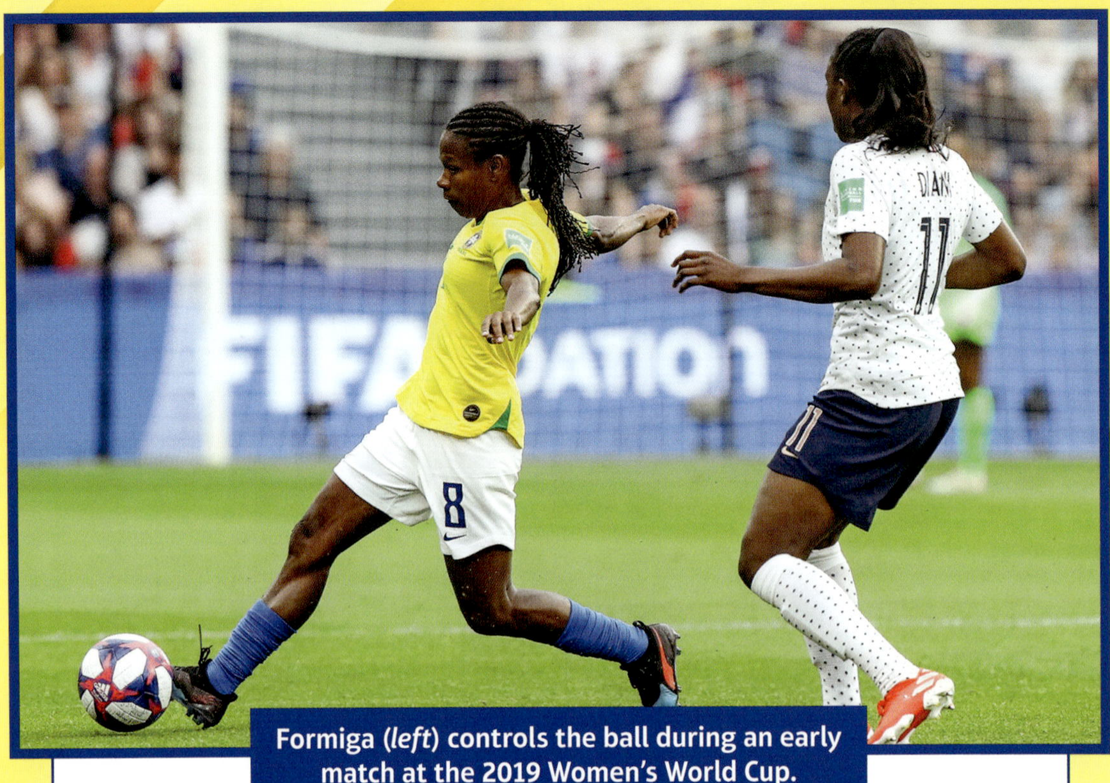

Formiga (*left*) controls the ball during an early match at the 2019 Women's World Cup.

The team made it all the way to the third-place match of the tournament. The game went to penalty kicks. Formiga stepped up, took the team's final shot, and scored. Brazil won!

FORMIGA

***Formiga* means "ant" in Portuguese. Miraildes Maciel Mota earned that name for her teamwork on the pitch.**

In the 2007 Women's World Cup, star players Marta and Cristiane joined Formiga on the team. They crushed the United States 4–0 to advance to the final. Marta's creative footwork and fierce kicks earned the team two of the match's goals. They faced Germany in the final match but lost 2–0. Despite the loss, Marta had the most goals in the tournament to win the Golden Boot award.

In 2022, Brazil's women's team faced Colombia for the Copa América title. In the 37th minute of play, midfielder Debinha buried a penalty kick in the back of the net to win the game 1–0. It was Brazil's fourth title in a row.

Debinha (*third from left*) celebrates after scoring during the Copa América final match in 2022.

In the semifinals of the 2024 Olympics, the women's team beat Spain 4–2. Brazil's third goal showed amazing teamwork. Striker Adriana took a shot, hit the crossbar, and received the ball back from teammate Portilho. Adriana took another shot and scored. In the final match against the United States, Brazil lost 1–0.

Adriana (*right*) scores a goal in the semifinals at the 2024 Olympics.

Rafaelle (*front*) takes a photo with fans at the 2024 Olympics.

CHAPTER 3

PASSIONATE PLAYERS AND FANS

If there is one word to describe Brazil's players and fans, it's passionate! The Country of Football has earned its nickname because of its love and dedication to the sport. Soccer is, by far, the most popular sport in the country.

Fans cheer on Brazil at the 2023 Women's World Cup.

Kids of all ages play soccer in Brazil. When Brazil plays in a World Cup, much of the country shuts down so that fans can watch their team play. At Maracanã Stadium in Rio de Janeiro, bright yellow and blue shirts fill the stands. Huge crowds of passionate fans sing, chant, and stand on their feet in support of Canarinho.

WORLD CUP HOST

Brazil is set to host the Women's World Cup in 2027. It will be their first time hosting the event.

Brazil's teams have a history of strong and talented players. The beautiful game they play captures the hearts of fans and leads them to victory. In upcoming World Cup tournaments, Brazil's loyal fanbase will cheer them on!

Brazil's women's team wins the silver medal at the 2024 Olympics.

BRAZIL WOMEN'S TEAM TIMELINE

1982 Brazil forms an official national women's soccer team.

1986 Brazil plays its first official international match against the United States.

1991 Brazil finishes ninth in the first Women's World Cup.

1999 Brazil finishes third at the Women's World Cup.

2004 Brazil wins the Olympic silver medal.

2007 Brazil finishes second at the Women's World Cup.

2008 Brazil wins the Olympic silver medal.

2022 Brazil wins its eighth Copa América title.

2024 Brazil wins the Olympic silver medal.

BRAZIL MEN'S TEAM TIMELINE

1914 Brazil plays its first official international match against England.

1919 Brazil wins its first South American Championship.

1958 Brazil wins its first Men's World Cup.

1962 Brazil wins its second Men's World Cup.

1970 Brazil wins its third Men's World Cup.

1994 Brazil wins its fourth Men's World Cup.

2002 Brazil wins its fifth Men's World Cup.

2019 Brazil wins its ninth Copa América.

GLOSSARY

crossbar: the horizontal bar on top of the goalposts

FIFA: a group that oversees soccer around the world

friendly match: a game played for fun and practice that isn't part of a larger competition

hat trick: when a player scores three goals in one game

midfielder: a soccer player who usually stays in the middle of the field

penalty kick: a free kick at the goal allowed for certain fouls or to decide the winner of some games

pitch: a soccer field

rivalry: when a player or team tries to defeat or be more successful than another

semifinal: the round of a tournament that determines which teams will advance to the final

striker: a soccer player whose main job is to score goals

LEARN MORE

Britannica Kids: Pelé
https://kids.britannica.com/kids/article/Pel%C3%A9/390829

Buckley, James. *Who Was Pelé?* Penguin Workshop, 2023.

Kiddle: Brazil National Football Team Facts for Kids
https://kids.kiddle.co/Brazil_national_football_team

Kiddle: Marta (footballer) Facts for Kids
https://kids.kiddle.co/Marta_(footballer)

Leed, Percy. *Pelé: Soccer Hero*. Lerner Publications, 2022.

Lilley, Matt. *The FIFA World Cup*. Apex, 2023.

INDEX

Copa América, 7–8, 20, 23

fans, 4, 10, 18, 25–27
Formiga, 22–23

Garrincha, 17–18
Germany, 14, 19, 23

Italy, 4, 18–19

Maracanã Stadium, 26
Marta, 5, 14, 23

Neymar, 20

Olympics, 7, 14, 20, 24

Pelé, 5, 11, 16–19

Sissi, 21

United States, 12, 14, 23–24

PHOTO ACKNOWLEDGMENTS

Image credits: Heidtmann/picture alliance via Getty Images, p. 4; Jerry Cooke/Sports Illustrated via Getty Images, p. 6; Brad Smith/ISI/Getty Images, p. 7; Popperfoto via Getty Images, pp. 8, 16; Historic Collection/Alamy, p. 9; AFP via Getty Images, p. 10; Horstmüller/Süddeutsche Zeitung Photo/Alamy, p. 11; David Cannon /Allsport/Getty Images, p. 12; MIKE FIALA/AFP via Getty Images, p. 13; Paul Gilham/Getty Images, p. 14; Ben Radford/Getty Images, p. 15; AP Photo/Kurt Strumpf, p. 17; Rolls Press/Popperfoto via Getty Images, p. 18; Bernd Weissbrod/picture alliance via Getty Images, p. 19; Laurence Griffiths/Getty Images, p. 20; Jon Buckle/EMPICS via Getty Images, p. 21; Zhizhao Wu/Getty Images, p. 22; Gabriel Aponte/Getty Images, p. 23; SYLVAIN THOMAS/AFP via Getty Images, p. 24; Juan Manuel Serrano Arce/Getty Images, p. 25; George Hitchens/SOPA Images/LightRocket via Getty Images, p. 26; Ayman Aref/NurPhoto via Getty Images, p. 27. Design elements: Ralf Hiemisch/Getty Images; Rifqyhsn Design/Getty Images; cunfek/Getty Images; poo worawit/Getty Images.

Cover: Mirko Kappes/picture-alliance/dpa/AP Images (left); Lucas GabrielCardoso/AG IF/AP Images (right).